↑LEAD WELL

Seven Dimensions of Wellness
for Women in Leadership

LEAD WELL

Seven Dimensions of Wellness
for Women in Leadership

PAULA WALKER KING, MD, MPH

LEAD WELL
Published by Purposely Created Publishing Group™
Copyright © 2019 Paula Walker King
All rights reserved.

No part of this book may be reproduced, distributed or transmitted in any form by any means, graphic, electronic, or mechanical, including photocopy, recording, taping, or by any information storage or retrieval system, without permission in writing from the publisher, except in the case of reprints in the context of reviews, quotes, or references.

Unless otherwise indicated, scripture quotations are from the Holy Bible, King James Version. All rights reserved.

Scriptures marked AMP are taken from the Amplified Version®. Copyright © 2015 by The Lockman Foundation. All rights reserved.

Printed in the United States of America

ISBN: 978-1-64484-006-1

Special discounts are available on bulk quantity purchases by book clubs, associations and special interest groups. For details email: sales@publishyourgift.com or call (888) 949-6228.
For information log on to www.PublishYourGift.com

Just prior to writing of this book, my parents transitioned from this earthly life, four months apart. This book is dedicated to my loving parents, Mr. Paul R. Walker, Sr. and Mrs. Dorothy Daniel Walker. Everything I am, I owe it all to you. Mama and Daddy, you gave me your best so that I could be the best and fully self-actualize. I could never repay you for all the love, kindness, encouragement and support that you showered upon me throughout my life. I'm thankful and grateful to God that I had the good fortune to be loved, raised, and nurtured by such wonderful human beings and stellar models of excellence-in-action. You taught me to dare to be different, to express myself, to be good to myself and to be true to myself. Thank you for loving me. Thank you for the countless words of wisdom and strategies for successfully navigating life's path and for cheering me on to follow my dreams and to live my best life—one that's punctuated with a sense of fulfilled purpose, joy, and most of all, wellness. I will cherish you always, Mama and Daddy, and carry the memory of you in my heart. Without a doubt, having you as parents has been the best thing that's ever happened to me!

Table of Contents

Foreword ix

Preface xv

Introduction 1

The Amalgamation of Favorable Health Components Equals Wellness 15

The Seven Dimensions of Wellness 17

    1. Physical Wellness 19

    2. Mental Wellness 45

    3. Spiritual Wellness 59

    4. Emotional Wellness 73

    5. Social (or Relational) Wellness 83

    6. Occupational Wellness 93

    7. Financial Wellness 101

Putting It All Together 109

About the Author 111

Foreword

There are four human challenges that unite us as human beings: financial challenges, relationship challenges, personal identity challenges and health challenges. In her debut book, *Lead Well: Seven Dimensions of Wellness for Women in Leadership*, Dr. Paula Walker King offers pragmatic insights into how we can center ourselves as women in a stress-driven culture; to find solutions to these areas of challenges; surmount obstacles; manage stress; and to maintain balance in the process.

A well-informed health practitioner, Dr. Walker King's debut book offers insightful dialogue that encourages, empowers, and educates.

Dr. Walker King is an amazing thought leader. Over the years of knowing her, I've had the pleasure of witnessing the growth and development of her personal and professional brand as a physician, caregiver, public speaker, and wellness expert.

As a wellness expert, extraordinary emergency medicine physician, professor, and consultant, Dr. Walker King understands that present-day womanhood generally means juggling multiple tasks and roles that include the roles we play as spouse, mother, industry, and community leader, etc. The truth is, it is a daunting task to add to our list of things-to-do, the maintenance of proper physical and emotional health while simultaneously navigating our active, on-the-go lifestyles.

As women, we often lessen our self-care regimen and physical fitness efforts for the "trade up" of caring for others while expending an already-taxed supply of energy needed to climb the proverbial ladder-of-career-success.

More than any other time in history, women are being called to lead in unprecedented ways and in nontraditional industries. While the rate of women in leadership roles is skyrocketing, so is the pressure to perform at almost superhuman levels. As a result, many women become overwhelmed and exhausted, which can often translate into unhealthy eating habits, lack of exercise, and an ever diminishing time slot for self-care.

In *Lead Well*, Dr. Paula Walker King is on a mission to help women from all walks of life to achieve optimum health. This book shares her experiences as an emergency medicine physician. It also highlights her empathy for a world filled with pain, provides practical principles for managing stress, and offers timeless wisdom, life strategies, and practical solutions to mitigate the tug-of-war between domestic and professional responsibilities and self-care; something that most women experience throughout their adult lives.

Lead Well is a practical guide to reconnecting to our inherent feminine nature as strategists, decision-makers, and influencers of our families, communities, and the workplace while creating emotional and physical vitality, mental clarity, and the overarching components of balance and optimum health so that we can remain both productive and prosperous in all areas of our lives.

As you read this timely book, may you live a long life filled with peace, happiness, and health as you learn to *Lead Well*.

Dr. N. Cindy Trimm
Life-Strategist, Author, Humanitarian

This book is for all women who serve in various roles, capacities and expressions of leadership.

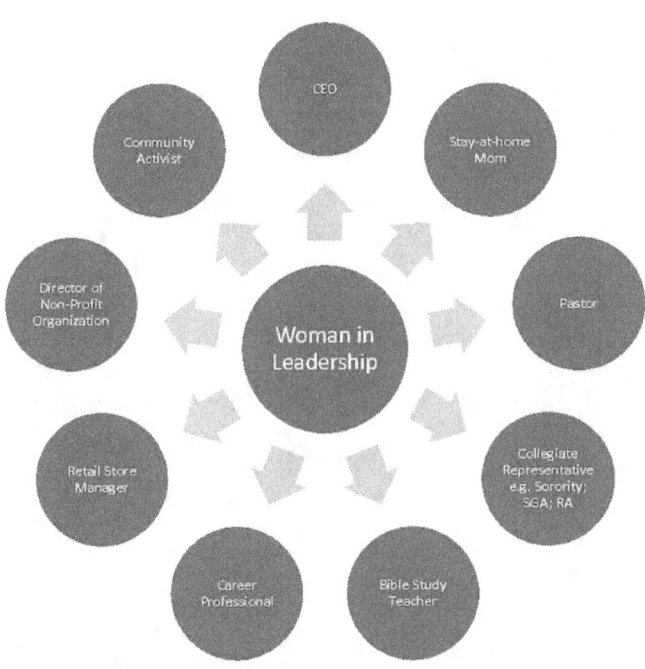

Preface

The wellness wisdom that is shared within these pages is so essential, like a required nutrient, that I've titled the corresponding coaching program for this book, W_2O, in the format of the chemical formula for water (H_2O). In this case, W_2O represents **W**isdom **to O**ptimize ™. In the W_2O program, I help facilitate your personal transformation in all seven dimensions of wellness.

Water, H_2O, is a macronutrient that's required by the body. In fact, water comprises 70 percent of the body and is the liquid milieu in which every biochemical reaction of the body takes place. The body's metabolism is the sum total of biochemical processes that occur to maintain life, and is dependent upon the presence of water. Without water, metabolism would be sluggish and insubstantial.

Likewise, the essential wisdom that's shared within the pages of this book and the corresponding coaching program, is essential for enjoying wellness and a state of balance in every dimension and phase of life. This book features the strategies and steps to empower women in leadership to lead well, spanning across the seven dimensions of wellness. I've had this message in my heart for years, and let the busyness of life interfere with penning this manuscript before now. It is my intention that this book will be a blessing to all that read it.

I am thankful for my wonderful and loving husband, Sam, for his support. He's the love of my life and I'm so grateful that God made him especially for me. I would like to thank my parents for encouraging the cultivation of my gifts and talents, and for equipping me with the skills to lead well. I thank my spiritual mom and mentor, Dr. Cindy Trimm, for all of her teachings, exemplary leadership, and encouragement. I extend a huge "thank you" to my Medical Mogul business coach, Dr. Draion Burch (Dr. Drai), for being a supportive guide and teacher and making sure that I wrote this book for once and for all. A huge shout out and thank you to Ms. Jai Stone, the Brand Mother, whom I affectionately call "Dr. Jai"; your advice was tremendously helpful. Last, but not least, I want to thank my family for their ongoing support, encouragement, and patience as I sowed many hours into the completion of this project. My heart is overjoyed and filled with gratitude.

Introduction

Wellness must be a priority for women leaders. Most women, even as little girls, assume roles that require us to be resourceful and creative problem-solvers. We are strategists, decision makers and influencers within our homes, communities, and workplaces. Typically, as a way of being and occurring, women befriend and tend. We befriend others easily and often, and seek out many opportunities for social engagement. Women also tend to take care of those entrusted to their care including spouses, children, aging parents, nieces, nephews, grandchildren, patients, clients, etc. Often, in the midst of making meaningful contributions to others, women neglect to engage in good self-care. We take care of other people but usually forget to take care of ourselves until it's too late, when an imbalance or dysfunction manifests.

As a doctor who's practiced Emergency Medicine and Population Medicine (public health) for over 10 years, I've seen my fair share of chronic disease exacerbations and advanced pathological states that are entirely preventable. Some are even reversible. The missing link is proper health education. People don't know what they don't know, and it's within these blind spots that people operate and make choices that are sometimes detrimental to health. Throughout my career, I find myself sharing health information with women of all ages, who want to better understand their bodies and how to take care of them. As a visionary, I know that if I can empower women to lead healthier lives, I can empower families and communities to live healthier. Typically when women receive strategy and information, as natural influencers and decision makers, they share the knowledge within the context of their families, communities and social circles. Fact: Teach a woman about nutrition, her family is going to eat healthier. That woman is going to ensure that the right foods are purchased and made available to her loved ones. So, although my message in this book is aimed toward women, my message is one that's intended to have intergenerational impact. I have a passion for providing health education to empower women to make better lifestyle choices. It is what drives my current career, practice, and research, but this wasn't always the case. It's been a long journey to discovering the elusive wisdom that activates greater capacities for optimized living so as to enjoy a heightened sense of vitality and well-being.

I was born in Atlanta, Georgia and grew up in Detroit, Michigan. I excelled academically throughout my school years and graduated at the top of my high school class. I left

Michigan and matriculated at Howard University as a Pre-Medicine student majoring in microbiology with a minor in chemistry. I graduated with honors from Howard University and was accepted into medical school back in Michigan, where I continued to excel. At the conclusion of my studies, I became the first physician in my family. I successfully matched and was selected for residency training at one of the nation's premier Emergency Medicine residency programs.

There, I received pivotal training as a woman in leadership. I was the first African American resident physician and first female physician to matriculate and graduate from the Emergency Medicine program at St. John Hospital & Medical Center. While learning and honing my expertise in medicine, I trained with 23 men. I was the only woman in my cohort. Never before had I been confronted with so many "-isms": sexism, chauvinism, racism, misogynism; you name it. The experience was awesome! I didn't know my own strength prior to that season in my life. I learned to trust my intuition and assert myself in what felt like a hostile environment at the time. I spoke up for myself when boundaries were crossed. I advocated for patients' rights when it wasn't popular to do so. On any given day, at any time, I could hold my own with any of my male colleagues during professional discourse. Despite every trial, I emerged as a leader.

I acquired additional certifications and was one of the first resident physicians to take on a teaching role. Within the hospital, I taught several resuscitation courses: Advanced Trauma Life Support (ATLS); Advanced Cardiac Life Support (ACLS); and Pediatric Advanced Life Support (PALS). It was during this particular phase of my medical training that I found my voice and discovered a love for teaching and public speaking. Prior to speaking in this capacity, I hated public speaking and feared it. As time passed, the acceptance of more speaking engagements served as systematic desensitization of the aversion for public speaking. The fear dissipated and confidence came. Now, I'm a fearless speaker and teacher to large audiences, nationally and internationally, and I love it! I'm grateful for my education in a male dominated environment. It made me a warrior and contributes to the leader that I am today.

As a woman in leadership, I am confident. I know how to negotiate challenges and surmount obstacles. I know how to persevere. I know how to present my ideas and articulate my persuasions. In the face of a "no", I'm skilled at searching for the "yes" on the other side of it. I know how to create from nothing and make things happen. I also know the experience of having feminine leadership challenged or questioned. I know what it's like to be misunderstood and mischaracterized as a Lady Leader. Truly, I have a heart for women in leadership. I know those struggles intimately, including the challenge to lead well.

Since those earlier experiences and throughout my career, I've gone on to break barriers and blaze trails, to open doors and create opportunities for other women and minorities in medicine and beyond. I crafted three successful careers as a physician, professor, and media personality. I rode this wave of success for years and reached a pinnacle. I married my friend and soulmate. Together, we have a beautiful son. On the outside, I've had a perfect life. But there was a time when I wasn't happy. I wasn't happy because what they told me in medical school wasn't true. People don't present to the emergency department with only acute medical crises. In fact, chronic disease is what often drives contemporary emergency department usage, especially when people don't have access to healthcare or health insurance. Moreover, in the emergency room, patients have a host of behavioral, psychosocial, socioeconomic and other lifestyle issues that are contributing factors to their disease and distress, which were never discussed in medical school! For example, nutritional science matters, but as a subject, it isn't uniformly taught in all medical schools. This is such a travesty, as the nutritional status of an individual is the underpinning of all states of health and disease. However, in the 23 years of educational training that was required to become a physician, I didn't even encounter a brief overview of the subject. Moreover, medical school didn't prepare me for the toxic culture of medicine and the bureaucracy of American healthcare. Often, healthcare decisions and practices are influenced and shaped by those that don't provide direct patient care, that is to say, health insurers and hospital administrators. Sadly, sometimes profits are prioritized over people. With all of the unexpected adversities, I was quickly burning out.

I remember vividly a particular day in the ER when I had seen a bevy of patients, all of whom had preventable exacerbations of disease ranging from the hypertensive patient who was in the ER because he "ran out of his medication" to the acute asthmatic who had been noncompliant with treatment. Sitting at the desk in the ER in my green scrubs and white coat, sipping a cup of freshly brewed coffee with the chatter of nearby colleagues in the background, I thought to myself: this is not what I envisioned as my role in healthcare. This is not why I went to medical school—to see patients struggle with repeat episodes and flare-ups of chronic illnesses, offering them no cure, no hope, just the temporary palliation of symptoms. Adding insult to injury, I had 60+ hour work weeks; I was stressed, sleep-deprived and overworked with very little time to spend with my family and friends. I was not living what I preached: balance, wellness, and wholeness. I felt sad and stuck. I didn't know how to move forward. I didn't know how to help my patients beyond what I had been taught in medical school—that you treat disease with a prescription or a procedure (surgical), in essence, "a pill for every ill" approach.

On top of this career frustration, I lost my parents—the first loves of my life—four months apart. First my dad transitioned, then my mom. It was devastating. It felt as though my heart had shattered into a million irretrievable pieces. My dad was a loving, kind man and ardent supporter of mine; he loved me deeply. My mom was my original BFF (Best Friend Forever) and my first life coach. She taught me the fundamentals of relationships, life strategy, and essential wisdom to live a healthy and balanced life. Losing my parents, I was overwhelmed with grief. Again, I felt sad and stuck. I was losing weight. I wasn't eating. I wasn't sleeping. I was socially withdrawn. My usual intellectual pursuits no longer interested me and my focus was broken. In essence, I was broken and my ability to lead was significantly impacted. Hitting that "rock bottom" was my wake up call. I had to find a way to get back to good self-care so that I could be well and lead well. I had to find a way to reinvent a life I loved so I could get my "happy" back.

I began to pursue additional education and avenues for better self-care. I explored several complementary healing modalities including massage therapy, meditation, raw fruit and vegetable juicing, aromatherapy, Reiki, and therapeutic seasonal fasting, among others. I also took a plethora of courses in nutrition and holistic health. For the first time ever, I learned nutritional science and the fundamental role that it plays in the genesis of health (and disease). I learned about mind-body medicine. My world was transformed.

Since my initial expedition to research natural therapies, I've earned additional degrees and certifications beyond medical school and residency. I've established myself as a health ambassador and subject matter expert on wellness and prevention science. Now, I preach and teach wellness to populations and communities across nations. I'm happy. I make a difference in people's lives by showing them how to be well. By employing simple principles for the different dimensions of wellness, I was able to re-gain a state of balance, health, energy, vitality and wholeness. I'm re-invigorated. I'm re-invented. Now, I help women who are just like me when I was challenged in my pursuit to lead well, while engaged in the daily grind of career advancement and attempting to achieve work life balance. I help women prevent Empty Cup Syndrome: a diagnosis that involves attempting to enrich others while lacking adequate self-care, leading to a progressive decline in one's experience of wellness. I help women in power elevate their career and manage their personal challenges in order to experience a full and abundant life. I help people customize their lives to find the time and freedom to do the things that they really love and enjoy. Today, I am thrilled to be of service to humanity in such a transformative way. I coach women globally so that they can live their best life and be the best version of themselves.

Being your best starts with wellness. How well you are, determines how you perform and show up in life. Your wellness status determines how productive you are. Being well sets the stage and allows for the full and uninhibited expression of your talents and gifts. Being well facilitates the execution of your destiny and purpose. Today, I find great satisfaction helping women maximize their health and well-being so that the fullest expression of their gifts and talents may come forth and bless others.

The purpose of this book is to share the seven dimensions of wellness and interventions that are designed to facilitate greater vitality and an optimized sense of well-being. Unlike conventional medicine, holistic healthcare aims to treat the whole person, including the various dimensions of life in which we all function—mind, body and spirit. Holistic healthcare emphasizes prevention above treatment and is oriented toward healing (cure) rather than merely the palliation of symptoms of disease. Additionally, in the holistic model when disease does occur, it is of paramount importance to uncover the etiology to assess the root (cause) and fruit (symptoms) of disease and imbalance.

This book is my gift to the women leaders of the world who may suffer with chronic illness—albeit physical or mental—in the face of other socio-contextual determinants and risk factors for disease. This book is for women leaders whose experience of wellness has been temporarily interrupted or impacted by a deluge of stressors, who need the blueprint for getting back in balance.

Once chronic illness strikes, conventional medicine typically offers little hope for disease regression or cure. Instead, serial doctor visits and routine medication management become the norm for those with chronic illnesses. Apathy often follows while most women become cynical and resigned to living with the illness or dysfunction for the remainder of their lives. This book will shine a light on the often overlooked behaviors, determinants and other contributing risk factors for disease that can be mitigated with simple interventions and a sincere intention to live a healthier and better life. Lady Leaders, there is hope. You can manifest wellness in every area of your life. In this book, I'll share with you:

- How health is multi-factorial
- How wellness is multi-dimensional

- How the mind-body-spirit continuum works
- The role spirituality plays in the experience of optimal health
- A brief overview of the scientific underpinnings of the mind-body connection and the role it plays in the formation of health and disease

Also, in this book, psychoneuroimmunology, the science that examines the relationships between the mind (psyche), brain (neuro), immune system (immunology) and their interrelated impact on healing the body will be briefly described. You will learn how to augment your nutrition for more vibrant, energetic health and how to maintain optimal nutrition for sustained healthy living. I will share how thoughts, feelings, beliefs and perceptual interpretations of experiences can influence well-being and how to deal more effectively with stress, including techniques for achieving balance mentally, physically, spiritually, and emotionally.

This book is intended to represent a compilation of wisdom and strategies that align us with the universal laws that govern health and wellness. In essence, there are certain non-negotiable principles of wellness that must be abided in order to obtain and achieve optimum energy and well-being.

The essential principles that are espoused and discussed in this book are time honored and proven principles that when employed amplify and support human health and accelerate it to an optimum expression known as wellness. To gain a deeper understanding of wellness, and what it is, let's first deconstruct the notion of wellness by examining a related concept—health.

What is Health?

If I were to survey 100 people and ask what is health, I would garner 100 different responses. Some would say: "Health means I don't have any pain or discomfort in my body." Others would say: "Health is a state of not having a diagnosed illness." Other definitions of health that a survey might yield include:

- Health is to feel good and energized.
- Health is to have no previous personal history of illness or family history of disease.
- Health is to be symptom-free.
- Health is to have all of your baseline tests and diagnostic labs on an annual physical exam return normal.

- Health is to be able to execute activities of daily living without difficulty.
- Health is to have a positive outlook on life and balanced mood and emotions.

The list goes on and on. Essentially, one's opinion of health is variable depending on who you're asking.

The Amalgamation of Favorable Health Components Equals Wellness

As our understanding of human health has evolved, additional health factors and dimensions of wellness are now observed in population medicine, including financial wellness, which is critical. After all, nothing deteriorates health quicker than the experience of debt stress, overwhelm and anxiety. As a doctor, what I know for sure is that health is multi-factorial. There is no singular component to what constitutes health. In other words, health is a combination of elements, variables, and different factors that synergistically work together for the benefit of the whole human organism. We are complex beings with several aspects to our nature. We are physical beings. We are spiritual. We are intellectual. We are interactive and relational. We're occupational and have careers and workplace dynamics to negotiate. If I were to describe health as on a continuum, wellness would be the highest expression of health. There are seven dimensions of wellness: physical, intellectual, spiritual, emotional, social, occupational, and financial. We will explore all seven dimensions of wellness in this book.

When concerted efforts are made to address and maximize the different components and capacities of health, an experience of wellness or optimized functionality and vibrancy result. Wellness is the desired outcome for all. Being well is your wealth. Like a water well, you can draw from the state of being optimally well to fuel and energize your efforts and expressions across the dimensions of life, over the span of your life. For it is when you're well in every dimension of your life, that you live the life that you were created to live and your body serves as a vehicle for the ultimate expression of your gifts.

Now, let's take a closer look at each of the different dimensions of wellness. Along the journey, I offer specific wisdom and strategies for each dimension that can be applied to optimize your vigor and vim for enhanced self-expression and an energized leadership style.

The Seven Dimensions of Wellness

1. PHYSICAL WELLNESS

Thomas A. Edison, the famous, brilliant visionary pioneer and inventor said, "The day is near at hand when the doctor will no longer be engaged to patch up the sick man, but to prevent him from getting sick... the doctor of the future will give no medicine, but will interest his patients in the care of the human frame, in diet and in the cause and prevention of disease." How prophetic and profound! Edison may not have realized at that time in the early 1900s that he was actually talking about wellness.

When most people think about their health, they often solely think about the physical plane of existence and the presence or absence of symptoms of disease. But physical health is a complex interplay of genes and environment. In this case, environment is the milieu in which genes operate to have their expression. This biological environment or milieu is often influenced by various lifestyle measures such as healthy or poor nutrition, the presence or lack of physical activity, certain habits such as smoking, alcohol consumption, recreational drug use, unmanaged stress, or sleep deprivation. This internal environment affects and alters how our genes are expressed. This concept alone is revolutionary. Until recent decades, it was thought that genes determined everything as it relates to our expression of health and wellness. Due to emerging data and increased research in the areas of nutrigenomics, psychoneuroimmunology and mind-body medicine, we now know that genetics has a bearing on about 30 percent of our health outcomes. Meanwhile, the primary drivers of our health and experience of well-being are our daily lifestyle choices, which represent approximately 70 percent of the health equation. This revelation is encouraging news! When it comes to health and its highest expression, wellness, genes do not equal destiny. Genes are not the primary determinants of health as we once believed. Daily lifestyle decisions, which are entirely under our control, largely determine our health outcomes, experience of well-being, and our ability to lead well.

For more than the last decade, heart disease, cancer, chronic respiratory diseases, stroke, and diabetes have been the leading causes of death for Americans. The common denominator shared by these health conditions is that they are preventable. In fact, almost all chronic diseases are preventable, and the trajectory of such disease is even reversible if intervention is begun early enough.

For example, Type II diabetes is a chronic disease that occurs in both adults and sedentary children and teens who are overweight. In the paradigm of prevention, the approach to addressing the signs and symptoms of diabetes would start at its pre-cursor state known as pre-diabetes. Intervention at the pre-diabetes stage would include the introduction of healthier eating habits and an exercise regimen that facilitates at least a ten percent loss of body weight. These simple lifestyle modifications can make the difference in whether there's full manifestation of the disease (diabetes) in those with risk factors alone, or whether the disease is treated with pharmaceutical therapy versus non-pharmaceutical interventions like daily exercise, weight loss/maintenance, stress mitigation, and diet. In this prevention scenario, we would be less likely to see the effects of end-stage brittle diabetes, which claims so many lives and impairs quality of life with accompanying end organ damage, e.g. eyes (blindness), heart (heart disease), and kidneys (kidney failure) that affects millions. Therefore, prevention is key.

In holistic healthcare, primary prevention of disease is the ideal goal. As part of this type of care, healthy individuals are counseled and educated about exercising, good nutrition, receiving recommended vaccinations, managing stress, wearing seatbelts and utilizing other safety precautions. Primary prevention, when practiced, has been shown to save lives and improve quality of life. So, why don't we practice prevention more vigorously?

In my professional experience as a physician and public health practitioner, I've noticed that apathy and discouragement are barriers to individuals practicing effective disease prevention. Too often, the mindset is that nothing can be done about a generational inheritance pattern of disease. After all, for decades medical scientists believed (and told the general public) that genes determined our biological destiny. If heart disease or diabetes were part of a family's history, developing those diseases seemed inevitable. However, thanks to a growing body of epigenetics research, we now know that genes do not equal destiny. While we cannot alter the structure of our genes or the sequence of our DNA, we can influence the expression of our genes to create good health and well-being. Through daily lifestyle choices, we can influence how our genes behave, helping to "turn on" the genes that promote good health and "turn off" or down regulate, the genes that promote illness.

WISDOM AND STRATEGIES TO OPTIMIZE YOUR PHYSICAL WELLNESS

The lifestyle interventions that are proven to matter most when creating physical wellness are:

1. Sleep

To lead well, we should be securing between seven and nine hours of sleep every night (preferably sleep that's not induced by alcohol or pharmaceuticals). Also, we should have a set bed time of 10:30 pm, no later than 11:00 pm. If we are in bed by this time, our chances are greater to secure the required sleep hours needed to be physically well in order to lead well. During deep sleep, the body releases accumulated stress and toxins while it self-regulates and repairs the cells of the body. If you're sleep deprived, you are more likely to have a weakened immune system and chronic inflammation, which is associated with many illnesses, including frequent colds or bouts of flu, Alzheimer's, fibromyalgia, autoimmune illnesses, and some forms of cancer.

2. Prayer/Meditation

Prayer and meditation represent a simple practice that takes us to a state of profound relaxation and dissolves fatigue and stress. People who pray and meditate regularly are less likely to develop high blood pressure, heart disease, anxiety, and other stress-related physical illnesses. I will talk more about this subject in the chapter on spiritual wellness.

3. Exercise/Physical Activity

Physical activity is any movement of skeletal muscle that occurs in an un-choreographed manner. Exercise, on the other hand, represents planned, intentional, repetitive and structured skeletal muscle movement intended to improve or exaggerate health and overall fitness. When it comes to human health, both planned intentional and structured movement (exercise) as well as unstructured skeletal muscle movement (physical activity) are beneficial to the body, with exercise yielding slightly greater benefits due to its intentional and repetitive nature which increases lean muscle mass by design.

In a general sense, we all know that exercise can help us lose weight and reduce belly fat. But did you know that you actually PAMPER yourself every time you exercise? For most, exercise does not conjure up luxuriating images or any sense of pleasure or self-indulgence. However, when you consider the benefits of exercise, you'll quickly understand why exercise/physical activity is one of the non-negotiable laws of health and the ultimate key to wellness.

As a physician and health educator, I shift paradigms. P.A.M.P.E.R. is an acronym that I created to teach the benefits of exercise so people would embrace this lifestyle intervention for greater endurance and energy to lead well. In the spirit of popular culture's successful milk campaign, exercise "does a body good!" This scientifically supported fact has led to the global health initiative called Exercise is Medicine®, which is managed by the American College of Sports Medicine (ACSM) and encourages physicians and other health care providers to include physical activity/exercise when designing treatment plans.

Earlier, I mentioned P.A.M.P.E.R. as a teaching tool and acronym to highlight the benefits of exercise. Indeed, you PAMPER yourself every time you engage in physical activity. Here's how exercise augments your health:

» **P** = **P**rotects you from heart disease

Regular workouts reduce your risk of cardiovascular problems such as high blood pressure and high levels of cholesterol and triglycerides. These conditions contribute to blocked or hardened arteries and contribute to heart disease, the number one killer of men and women in the U.S., according to the Centers for Disease Control and Prevention (CDC).

» **A** = <u>A</u>ge in reverse

Exercise can improve your health to the point where you look and feel younger than you are.

» **M** = <u>M</u>emory is enhanced

With regular exercise, you can fight brain fog and achieve enhanced mental clarity. Regular aerobic exercise seems to increase the size of the hippocampus, a part of the brain associated with memory. Additionally, exercise is linked to sharper cognitive skills.

P = <u>P</u>osture is improved

With advancing age, poor posture can develop due to muscle loss and bone density changes. You can counteract this tendency with exercise and strength training, which builds muscle and bone mass, especially in your core and along your spine, so you naturally stand taller and shave years off your appearance.

» **E** = <u>E</u>nergizes

Exercise gives you more energy. It also increases your libido (sex drive).

»

> **R** = **R**elieves stress and musculoskeletal pain

Exercise relieves stress and can, in some instances, relieve musculoskeletal pain. Physical therapy in patients with injuries and accompanying pain is a good example of this latter concept. Moreover, endorphins are released when we exercise. Endorphins, also known as endogenous morphine or internally produced morphine, are our body's natural "feel good" hormones and they heighten our overall sense of well-being, causing us to feel pain-free and less stressed.

Your body is engineered for movement and regular exercise is a key to health and longevity. The benefits of regular physical activity are too numerous to be constrained by my P.A.M.P.E.R. acronym, including: increased muscle mass, improved bone density (healthier bones), and better glucose tolerance (decreased risk for diabetes). Not only does exercise keep the body young and strong, it also preserves the brain's ability to learn, adapt, and perform other cognitive tasks (neuroplasticity).

To enjoy these benefits of exercise and many more, please talk with your doctor before beginning an exercise regimen. He/she can give you a customized exercise prescription that you can safely follow to P.A.M.P.E.R. yourself and derive all of the health enhancing benefits of exercise to optimize your physical wellness and ability to lead well.

4. Optimal Nutrition

The key to optimal nutrition is to favor a variety of fresh, whole foods including plenty of vegetables, whole grains, fruits, and herbs—while eliminating refined, processed foods, which are stripped of vital nutrients and contain a lot of sugar, artificial ingredients, and other harmful chemicals. Processed foods are a major source of chronic inflammation, which is an underlying cause of many serious diseases. Alternatively, whole, fresh foods decrease inflammation and provide valuable vitamins, minerals, and fiber.

In addition to whole foods, healthy fats are necessary for physical wellness. Although fats are often maligned and misunderstood, there are many healthy fats that are beneficial and supportive of optimal physical wellness. You may be surprised to learn that some fats are necessary for good health.

The human body is composed of trillions of cells. Within the cell membrane of each of those cells is Omega-3 fatty acids. Scientists have found that the essential fatty acids identified as Omega-3 are vital to well-being. In nutritional science, when the term *"essential"* is used, it refers to a substances that the body cannot produce. Therefore, in order to have the "essential" dietary substances or nutrients available as raw materials for building health, you must consume them in the foods you eat. Omega-3 fatty acids are not substances the body naturally produces. Therefore, in order to acquire the Omega-3 fatty acids required for optimal health, you will need to consume foods containing them. There are three types of Omega-3 fatty acids: alpha-linolenic acid (ALA), eicosapentaenoic acid (EPA), and docosahexaenoic acid (DHA). Neither of the Omega-3 fatty acids is produced in sufficient volume alone to support optimal human health. Eating foods rich in these nutrients along with dietary supplementation is necessary for maximum health outcomes.

Whole foods that contain healthy fats, such as nuts, seeds, and avocado are excellent sources of Omega-3 fatty acids to catapult your experience of physical wellness. Other food sources that provide ample amounts of Omega-3 fatty acids are:

- Salmon and mackerel
- Eggs (the yolks contain the most Omega-3)
- Flaxseed
- Walnuts
- Leafy vegetables
- Fortified foods e.g. milk, yogurt, etc.

Omega-3 fatty acids help enhance the body's immune system functioning along with the health of the joints; they also contribute to cardiovascular, eye, skin, and brain health. Nutritional science suggests that the benefits of omega-3s include reducing the risk of heart disease and stroke. Additionally, Omega-3 fatty acids are beneficial in relieving the symptoms of hypertension, joint pain and other rheumatologic problems, as well as certain skin ailments like eczema and psoriasis. It is recommended that every adult female (and male) consume at least 1000 milligrams (or 1 gram) of Omega-3 daily. If you don't eat enough of the foods that contain Omega-3 fats, dietary supplementation is always an option to ensure your body has the nutrition it needs.

Fats have higher caloric content than carbohydrates and proteins. However, as I just shared, our physical wellness wouldn't be optimized without certain healthy fats being incorporated into the diet. Because of their higher caloric content, fats are so often mischaracterized and maligned in the media that the therapeutic nature of certain fats is entirely missed. In fact, many food manufacturers will go so far as to produce fat-free processed foods. However, many fat-free and low-fat processed foods are loaded with added sugars and/or salt to replace the missing fat, which makes them not-so-healthy options. If you're trying to cut calories, don't eliminate the Omega-3 foods. Those can be regarded as good calories, meaning the benefit-risk ratio for Omega-3 foods is skewed in the direction of benefit. So, keep those as part of your diet and instead, cut out the unhealthy fats from your diet, such as the saturated and trans fats, which compose the standard American diet: hamburgers, French fries, steak, chicken, cookies, cakes, etc.

If you're wondering about low-fat dietary options in general, the best low-fat foods are low-fat plain milk, Greek yogurt, vegetables, fruits; and 100% whole grains such as bread, nuts and unsweetened cereals.

5. Increase Water Consumption

No discussion of optimal physical wellness would be complete without including the importance of hydrating with water. I specifically note hydration with water as critical for health and wellness because in this era of convenience and bottled beverages, people tend to hydrate with other non-equivalent fluids such as bottled fruit juices, Kool-Aid, Gatorade, Powerade, lemonade and the infamous Southern sweet tea. Erroneously, it is assumed that drinking these alternative beverages is equivalent to rehydrating the body, which is false. All of these options are poor substitutes for what our body really craves—pure, unadulterated water. Our bodies are 70% water. We're constantly borrowing from our water reserves via perspiration, urination, lacrimation (the formation of tears), inhalation and exhalation, where small amounts of water evaporate from the surface of the lungs during each respiratory cycle, as well with the production of digestive juices that are utilized to process and adequately metabolize our foods. Consequently, these water stores need to be replaced through rehydration practices that strategically occur across the span of each day. We have to make a conscious effort to hydrate with water in order to have the energy, mental clarity and stamina to lead well. Here's where apps and other reminders may come in handy. We benefit from the assistance of hourly reminders to drink water since our body's signal for thirst tends to decrease as we age. You may have noticed in your own life that you can go all day, or longer, without water but rarely go long periods without food. That's because of the waning thirst signals with advancing age, along with the phenomenon of sometimes confusing thirst with hunger as we get older. So, hydrate, hydrate, hydrate for optimal physical wellness.

So, how much water should be consumed daily? As a rule of thumb, take your weight in pounds and divide it by two, not to exceed one (1) gallon per day. Dividing your weight by two helps determine how many ounces of water you should drink daily. For example, a 125-pound person, should consume at least 63 ounces of water per day. There are eight ounces in a glass. Therefore, a 125-pound individual should consume approximately eight (8) glasses of water per day.

Increasing water consumption, in small sips, across the span of the day is the best way to avoid the untoward effect of consuming large volumes of water all at once with repeat trips to the bathroom to urinate. Easy does it. A few sips of water each hour is helpful in maintaining steady hydration. Eventually, your body will adjust to your newfound hydration practice and make the shift. Water is an essential macronutrient and plays a role in metabolism. Every biochemical reaction in the body takes place in the presence of water. Water also assists with regulating body temperature, transporting nutrients and oxygen to cells, removing cellular waste, and cushioning joints. Surprisingly, water is needed for the efficient manufacture of neurotransmitters, including serotonin, which contributes to a positive mood and elevated sense of well-being. As such, water is directly connected to healthy cognitive functioning and helps prevent memory loss and brain fog as we age.

I can't stress hydrating with water enough to maximize physical wellness. Up to 75 percent of Americans may be functioning in a chronic state of dehydration. Some of the common ailments that are linked to dehydration might surprise you. Headaches is one of the most common signs of dehydration. If you notice your skin is constantly dry and lacks elasticity, it could be a sign that your body is lacking water. Your skin is your body's largest organ and it needs water in order to stay healthy. Believe it or not, constipation is a sign of dehydration. Gastrointestinal transit time decreases with dehydration and the bowels move more sluggishly leading to constipation. As I mentioned earlier, sometimes thirst is confused with hunger, especially in adults. When the body is dehydrated, it can mistakenly send false hunger signals to the brain instead of thirst signals.

One major symptom that is caused by dehydration and negatively impacts our ability to lead well is fatigue. If you find that you are sleepy, tired, and fatigued all the time it could be a sign of dehydration. When the body lacks water, it can lower blood pressure and limit the oxygen supply to the brain. This creates a feeling of lethargy and sleepiness. Staying hydrated is one of the easiest ways to remain alert and energized throughout the day.

Water is necessary to maintain healthy joints and cartilage. In fact, the joints and cartilage of the body are made up of approximately 80% water. When your body lacks water, it can cause desiccation of cartilaginous joints, which produces friction in the joints leading to pain.

Dehydration can also have a huge impact on how your heart functions. When you drink less water, it causes a decrease in blood plasma, which makes your blood more viscous—and viscous blood is more prone to blood clot formation. As the blood thickens, it makes your heart work harder to circulate blood throughout the body, leading to an accelerated heart rate and increased blood pressure. Therefore, you should be drinking at least half of your body weight in water per day, not to exceed a gallon per 24-hour period.

To avoid dehydration, make water your beverage of choice. Every healthy adult should consider the following:

- Travel with water where possible to encourage consumption

- For maximum hydration, limit intake of energy drinks and caffeinated beverages. I know a lot of Lady Leaders that rely on coffee to give energy surges and boosts to mental clarity and functioning. However, caffeine is a natural diuretic that causes water loss and will precipitate dehydration if you're not implementing measures to rehydrate.

- Consider hydrating before, during, and after exercise. Exercise exaggerates water losses as a result of increased perspiration.

6. Massage Therapy

The ancient scrolls declare that "we are fearfully and wonderfully made" (Psalm 139:14 KJV). I continue to be fascinated with the innumerable healing capacities of the human body. Within the skin, there's a pharmacy of biochemical substances that are liberated when the skin is manipulated through massage. These biochemical substances include endorphins and other chemicals that exert an anti-inflammatory effect, keeping us healthy and less prone to chronic disease. When the skin is manipulated through massage, the lymphatic vessels, which are sandwiched between skeletal muscles, are also massaged and given an opportunity to detoxify and rid themselves of waste-laden lymph fluid, full of toxins and impurities. That's why it's important to hydrate and drink plenty of water immediately following a massage to flush out toxins and to rehydrate skeletal muscles to allow for greater flexibility and ease of skeletal muscle movement. If you've ever had a massage, you've probably recognized the familiar practice where the massage therapist offers a glass of water immediately after the massage concludes to flush out recently released impurities and toxins.

The lymphatic system is intimately connected to the immune system. Massage therapy nurtures and supports the health of the lymphatic system. When the lymphatic system is healthy, the immune system is healthy and better prepared to fight disease on our behalf.

Simply put, the immune system has been engineered to detect self (or that which is native to the body) versus non-self (a health threat that shows up post nativity). For example, your healthy body represents your native self. Non-self entities include bacteria, viruses, parasites, fungi and even a mutated cell. When any of these non-self entities show up, the immune system is designed to orchestrate an elaborate response to annihilate the potentially health and life threatening pathogen.

In some quirky instances, the immune system becomes confused and turns on itself in what's called an autoimmune illness. Examples of autoimmune illness include lupus (systemic lupus erythematosus), rheumatoid arthritis, and a type of hyperthyroid condition known as Graves' disease to name a few.

In the case of the mutated cell (the origin of cancer), a healthy and properly functioning immune system is responsible for destroying that mutated cell, robbing the malignant cell of an opportunity to proliferate to form other abnormal or cancerous cells, which if unchecked leads to tumor formation (cancer). In sum, cancer development is the result of an underlying immune system dysfunction. More specifically, the concept is known as cancer immunoediting, which is the immune basis of malignancy. This is the process by which cancer cells evade immunologic surveillance, bypassing the immune synapse and are no longer recognized as non-self antigens. Keeping the immune system healthy and supported through adjunctive lifestyle measures is imperative to our experience of physical wellness.

Within the human body, there are four pathways of elimination and detoxification. The skin is the largest organ of the body and it represents a pathway of excretion and elimination by way of perspiration. The lungs are another pathway for elimination through the cycles of inhalation and exhalation. We breathe in oxygen, which is utilized by the trillions of cells that make up our body and breathe out (eliminate) carbon dioxide—a waste product for humans, but an essential raw material for the botanical world that's used during the process of photosynthesis. Following the lungs, the kidneys are the third pathway of elimination and detoxification for the body allowing for the releasing of toxins, wastes, and impurities through urination. Lastly, the colon is the fourth site of elimination and detoxification, allowing for the passage and excretion of wastes through defecation.

The skin is heavily engaged during massage therapy and when accompanied by deep breathing, yields significant detoxification through this healing modality when done regularly. In order to lead well, weekly massage should become a component of your self-care regimen. Massage therapy is one of the oldest healing art forms that exerts exceptional therapeutic benefit to the physical body and causes one's experience of wellness to soar.

7. Healthy Emotions

Every emotion and thought you entertain affects your health. Put simply, there's a chemical messenger that's assigned to every thought and emotion that you have, which exerts subsequent effects on both the nervous system and the immune system.

The discipline of psychoneuroimmunology provides rich evidence that the body is deeply affected by moods and negative emotions. We know for sure that chemical messengers convey the energy and language of our emotions. When a person feels fear or anxiety, the body responds with the fight-or-flight response, releasing chemical messengers (hormones). These chemical messengers exert their effects on the body's organ systems in the face of fear, elevating heart rate and blood pressure and increasing the production of cortisol, adrenaline, and other so-called stress hormones.

Living in a state of chronic stress, where the fight-or-flight axis is activated frequently, can lead to increased inflammation in the body and the development of various states of imbalance or disease. Conversely, when you manage your stress and cultivate healthy emotions, you promote self-healing, self-regulation, and balance in the body.

These advancements in our scientific awareness and understanding of emotions and their impact on physical wellness are transformational. I share these insights with the hope that as leaders you'll be mindful of how the mind body connection works. Emotions and thoughts are things; they shape our decisions and drive our behaviors. The notion of a healthy thought life is corroborated by the ancient scripture in Philippians 4:8 of the Bible, which states "…whatever is true, whatever is honorable and worthy of respect, whatever is right and confirmed by God's word, whatever is pure and wholesome, whatever is lovely and brings peace, whatever is admirable and of good repute; if there is any excellence, if there is anything worthy of praise, think continually on these things [center your mind on them, and implant them in your heart] (Amplified Version of Bible)."

In this section on physical wellness, we've covered several important features to increase our ability to lead well. I encourage you to take charge of your health! Genetics only represents 30 percent of the health equation. The other 70 percent that determines how well you are, is determined by lifestyle—the choices you make each and every single day.

No longer do you have to accept the notion that just because Big Mama had diabetes and Daddy had diabetes that eventually you, too, will have diabetes. This thought process and premise is outdated and couldn't be further from the truth. We get to choose wellness or dis-ease (a lack of ease) as our way of being. Each day, each choice exerts a compound effect on overall health. So, why not choose life? Why not choose wellness? Genes do not equal destiny. Disease and disability are not inevitable. Activate your genes now for good health and wellness by implementing these simple wisdom measures and practice them consistently on a daily basis. The power is in your hands to lead well. So, take back your health and live your best life yet!

Reflections

Reflections

Reflections

2. MENTAL WELLNESS

The intellectual dimension of wellness envelops the domain of the mind and its accompanying thoughts, imagination, impressions, and visions. The auspices of intellectual wellness (or mental wellness) also include one's creativity and genius and the natural expression of one's God given talents and abilities. As leaders, the domain of the intellect is where we tend to thrive. On a daily basis, we're problem solving, we're creating, we're envisioning possibilities and expressing our genius. Being intellectually well means being naturally curious and imaginative, and often starts with the presence of a sound mind. When we're intellectually well, we're able to balance the vicissitudes of the mind and the ebb and flow of thoughts with ease, without experiencing encroaching anxiety or overwhelm. Intellectual wellness is synonymous with mental wellness. The strength of our mental health is very much connected to our overall state of physical well-being.

Stress is the biggest threat to our intellectual wellness. It is a disruptive mental health trigger. Stress can exert a huge impact on our lives and make the execution of occupations or activities of daily living difficult.

There are two types of stress. There's eustress and distress. Typically, when we think of stress, it has a negative connotation. The stress that results from a negative stressor is called distress. Examples of negative stressors that would result in distress include: death of a loved one, a divorce, financial worries or debt. On the other hand, sometimes stress results from a positive stressor or situation, such as an upcoming wedding or graduation where we may find ourselves stressed trying to attend to all of the details required for one of these events. Eustress is stress that results from a positive stressor. Interestingly enough, whether it's eustress (stress resulting from a positive stressor) or distress (stress resulting from a negative stressor), the impact on human physiology is the same. All stress activates a "fight or flight" response and causes several physiological changes to occur in the body including, but not limited to:

- Increased heart rate
- Increased blood pressure
- Increased respiratory rate with shallow breaths
- Vision and hearing become more acute
- Increased muscle tension
- Digestion stops because energy is needed to "fight or flee" the perceived threat and increased glucose

> (blood sugar) is released by the liver to serve as an energy source to "fight or flee" the stressor

Stress, when it's acute and self-limited, tends to invigorate the physiology like the proverbial adrenaline rush. However, stress that is chronic and prolonged tends to exert an injurious effect on the body, putting an individual at greater risk for physical illnesses such as high blood pressure, heart disease, diabetes and emotional eating, which leads to obesity.

WISDOM AND STRATEGIES TO OPTIMIZE YOUR MENTAL WELLNESS

The lifestyle interventions that are proven to matter most when creating mental wellness are:

1. **Carve out time to relax and rejuvenate regularly.** When we are relaxed, the physiological axis of the "fight or flight" response is deactivated causing the antithesis of the stress response to occur: normal blood pressure; normal heart rate; deeper, diaphragmatic breaths; additional glucose (blood sugar) is not released by the liver into the bloodstream and muscles are no longer tense and stiff. To lead well, beloved, you must carve out time each and every day to have fun and relax, even if it's only for 15-30 minutes each day. As I share this recommendation, I'm reminded of something my husband, Sam, said to me prior to our marriage. It was about 7 pm on this particular day, when Sam asked, "What are we going to do for fun today?" At the time, I had just worked a 12-hour day. Having fun was the farthest from my mind. I was looking forward to going home, having dinner, showering, and preparing for bed. When I replied to Sam that I had nothing fun planned for the day, he gasped in amazement. Sam quickly responded in a serious,

sage-like manner saying, "To work all day and not even take one hour to have fun to enjoy yourself means you've wasted an entire day of your life. Life is to be enjoyed. If you're not having fun, you're wasting the precious days of your life." Stunned at first, I quickly thought to myself, if Sam's metric for quality of life is to be embraced, then I had "wasted" a great number of my days being a passion-filled, productive, always-on-the-go leader. Fun had not been a priority, which was to my detriment, especially earlier in my career when I experienced symptoms of burnout. So glean this lesson from my story, Ladies, and take heed to Sam's advice. Have fun daily!

2. **Be a life-long learner.** As you remain curious and engage the brain in new activities and stimulation, you increase the neuronal reserve of the brain, also known as neuroplasticity. Neuroplasticity confers resiliency to the brain and its performance of cognitive tasks. Individuals with high neuroplasticity are more likely to rebound without residual deficit should a neuronal injury occur, such as a stroke. Neuroplasticity may also be protective against cognitive decline and certain forms of dementia like Alzheimer's. To increase your neuroplasticity, read at least 10 pages of a book daily; practice puzzles; learn a new language; enroll in a course; learn a new professional

skill. All of these lifestyle measures exert neuroprotective effects and preserve brain health.

3. **Healthy nutrition**, which was discussed in the previous section, is also a strategy for amplifying mental wellness, as well as physical wellness. A well balanced diet is infused with Omega-3 fatty acids, which are nutrients for brain and nerve cell health. Moreover, optimal nutrition has been linked to the hippocampus, a key area of the brain involved in learning, memory, and overall mental health. People who consume healthy diets have more hippocampal volume than those with unhealthy diets. As a wisdom strategy, eating more fruits, vegetables, whole grains, legumes, fish, olive oil, and other healthy foods while eating fewer processed foods can be an effective method for staving off mental health imbalance and depression.

4. **Engage in creative pursuits** such as music therapy. Play an instrument, write poetry, create artwork, crochet, or knit. Do anything that requires you to produce something or utilize your creativity and exhibit artistic self-expression. These artistic outlets are desirable for expanding your intellectual wellness. Engagement and execution of

one's natural expression of creativity stimulates the right hemisphere of the brain to become more creative. In essence, expressing creativity begets more creativity. Some of you have probably noticed that after traveling or immersing yourself in new experiences, there is a tendency to feel revived and rejuvenated in ways not previously experienced. Often, there is a tendency to have greater degrees of mental clarity and focus and to be more intellectually nimble, brimming with new thoughts and ideas. Engage in creative pursuits. It will do wonders for your intellectual wellness quotient.

5. **Exercise.** As, I mentioned in a previous section, exercise releases a surge of substances that are beneficial to physical health. Exercise also releases brain substances, or neurotransmitters, that play a pivotal role in brain health and hence, mental wellness, including serotonin, dopamine, and endorphins, which are like endogenous morphine substances making us feel well, relaxed, and pain-free. Endorphins are chemical messengers that are released when we experience stress or pain, to reduce the negative effects of each and to increase pleasure throughout the body. Endorphins are responsible for the euphoric feeling known as the "runner's high" that occurs after intense exercise. Serotonin is a neurotransmitter that

increases during exercise and yields psychological uplift and elevated mood as its effects. Low serotonin levels have been linked to generalized anxiety, depression, and Pre-Menstrual Syndrome (PMS). Dopamine is linked to mental health conditions, including depression and post-traumatic stress disorder, when levels of this brain substance or neurotransmitter are too low. Exercise boosts dopamine levels in the brain.

6. **Sleep** is fundamental to a healthy mind and body and overall mental wellness. Sleep deprivation and poor quality of sleep can increase the risk of developing signs and symptoms of mental health imbalance like irritability, paranoia, anxiety, and depression.

7. **Smile more. Laugh each and every day**. Gelotology is the study of laughter and its physiological and psychological effects on the body. Humor and optimism are good medicine and benefit several organ systems. Even the proverb says, **"A merry heart doeth good like a medicine" (Proverbs 17:22 KJV)**. Remember Sam's advice. "If you let a day go by without having fun, then you've wasted an entire day of your life." Make sure you enjoy good belly laughs while you're having fun, which engage the diaphragm and promote optimal relaxation.

As Lady Leaders, smiling more and laughing daily are natural stress busters that are easily accessible and readily available. Besides, our smiles are a part of our charm and allow us to more easily connect with those we lead.

8. **Good Time Management**. Nothing adds to stress levels and negatively impacts mental health like poor time management. When we neglect to leave enough time margin to accomplish tasks, we often feel rushed, harried, and stressed. As a wisdom strategy, incorporate larger allotments of time to accomplish tasks in a timely manner. Moreover, don't procrastinate. Procrastination is the assassination of divine inspiration. Have you ever noticed? You can have a witty idea or invention and then drag your feet with the execution phase. Before you know it, someone else has operationalized the idea. Again, procrastination is the assassination of divine inspiration. Be intentional about the use of each day that you are privileged to embrace. Use your time wisely. It all starts with 24-hours. Once you master the wise utilization of a day, you can master a week, a month, a year and so forth.

9. **Maintain a positive outlook**. Cheer and optimism create buoyancy in your intellectual style. You're able to

pivot and navigate challenges quickly and with agility. A positive outlook also fosters the spirit of gratitude, which increases your intellectual and emotional reserves and magnetizes you for serendipities and new opportunities.

Reflections

Reflections

Reflections

3. SPIRITUAL WELLNESS

As a doctor, who happens to be an ordained Christian minister, I am highly fascinated by the interrelationship of spiritual wellness to the other dimensions of wellness. The mind-body-spirit connection is a continuum that can't be severed. The mind impacts the body and spirit. Conversely, the spirit impacts the mind and body. When it comes to spiritual wellness, the domain of spirit exerts a causal effect and is very much related to our degree of feeling whole, happy, complete, and well. It's interesting to note that physical health and wellness are typically viewed through the lenses of the biomedical sciences. Historically, when considering science and spirituality, the two have been described in terms of being like oil and water—as if science and spirituality don't commingle. Increasingly, science is being shown to support historically held spiritual premises and beliefs. For example, in the ancient scrolls, it is declared "Beloved, I pray that in every way you may succeed and prosper and be in good health [physically], just as [I know] your soul prospers [spiritually]" (3 John 2 Amplified Bible). It sounds a lot like the dimensions of the holistic health model being described in this verse of scripture. Accepting this statement as true and extrapolating, we have been engineered by God, Lady

Leaders, with the intent in mind to prosper in every dimension of wellness: physically, spiritually, intellectually, occupationally, socially, financially, and emotionally.

Like health, spirit and spirituality mean different things to different people. So, I'm mindful that not all individuals share my Christian faith. However, what's remarkable to me is that within every spiritual tradition are similar tenets, such as the aforementioned statement, found in Christianity, Judaism, Islam, etc. No matter the spiritual discipline, I can locate a similar spiritual principle in the Bhagavad Gita, the Kaballah, and the Torah, among other spiritual texts. God is sovereign and His blueprint for health and wellness is iterative throughout the spiritual texts and traditions of the world.

While there is variance in how spirituality is expressed, one constant is the role of spirituality in health and optimized wellness. For example, centenarians have been studied vastly throughout the decades looking at the impacts of the power of belief, faith, prayer, mindfulness, meditation and a positive attitude, in the hopes of finding the key to longevity or the proverbial fountain of youth. In study after study across the globe, it has been repeatedly revealed that the common denominator among all centenarians, those living to age 100 and beyond, is that they all have some form of expressed faith or spirituality. This finding is very impactful as it suggests that spiritual wellness possibly plays a critically significant role in human longevity. Spirituality has additional utility for patients, especially when managing disease, confronting difficult diagnoses, and negotiating and supporting lifestyle changes.

WISDOM AND STRATEGIES TO OPTIMIZE YOUR SPIRITUAL WELLNESS

The lifestyle interventions that are proven to matter most when creating spiritual wellness are:

1. **Forgiveness.** Forgiveness has long been advocated as a virtue; something we ought to do because it is inherently good and the so-called "right thing to do". After all, there's a consensus and some semblance of the notion of forgiveness in almost all spiritual texts, traditions, and observations. Forgiveness is connected to improved outlook and has health implications. There's no one definition of forgiveness. But in general, forgiveness is a decision to let go of resentments and thoughts of revenge as the result of an offense. Forgiveness is the act of freeing yourself from self-sabotaging thoughts and feelings that bind you to an affront committed against you. It is important to note that forgiveness is not pardoning, excusing, or stating that an offense will be treated as acceptable behavior in the future. Forgiveness is not forgetting. Forgiveness is very much about remembering. In fact, one must recall and acknowledge negative emotions and events before forgiveness can occur. Futuristically, remembering also enables one to better self-protect and

keep clear and healthy boundaries moving forward in new situations and scenarios.

Forgiveness Is a Skill That You Build

Forgiveness is not something that necessarily comes easy for most. It is a skill that you build. It takes intentionality and effort to "let bygones be bygones". Lady Leader, it requires an incredible amount of energy to hold grudges. As long as you're using your precious energy to hold on to affronts and offenses, that's precious energy that's not being used to create the life of your dreams or wildest imagination. Energy that could otherwise be used to contribute to, or enhance one's existing state of health and well-being is otherwise squandered in thoughts of retaliation, anger, and bitterness. The following are critical distinctions about the skill of forgiveness:

- Forgiveness is, first and foremost, an internal process. It is primarily done by you, for you (no one else).

- Forgiveness is a path to freedom; it frees you from the sustained influence of the 'offender.'

- Forgiveness breaks patterns that would otherwise be repeated, interfering with existing relationships and sabotaging future relational wellness.

- Forgiveness need not require reconciliation. Just because you forgive someone doesn't mean that they earn a place in your inner circle. Quite the contrary, you can extend positive regard from afar. Or as my grandmother would say, "You feed them out of a long handled spoon," meaning the extension of forgiveness doesn't necessarily equate to exoneration or heightened proximity in relationship status.
- Forgiveness can take time and concentrated effort. It's not automatic.

Again, forgiveness is a skill you build. Like a muscle, the more you practice forgiveness and pardoning someone who has mistreated you, the more adept you become at this important life skill and strategy for experiencing optimal physical and spiritual wellness.

Over time, forgiveness becomes easier to do, especially when you stay present to the fact that forgiveness is the gift that you give yourself. In fact, forgiveness is the gift that keeps on giving. Here are the health benefits that have shown to be connected to the spiritual practice and discipline of forgiveness:

- lower blood pressure
- stress reduction

- decreased anxiety
- decreased symptoms of depression, hostility, and guilt
- decreased feelings of hurt, anger, and negative thoughts
- increased hope
- greater self-efficacy
- enhanced optimism
- increased physical vitality and quality of life
- decreased vulnerability to substance use and abuse and
- better overall mental, spiritual, and physical health and well-being

Forgiveness brings a peace that helps you progress in life. It keeps you from becoming stuck. The initial offense is no longer front and center in your thoughts or feelings. It's important to remember that forgiveness often isn't a one-time act. It begins with a decision, but because memories, words, or actions of others may trigger old feelings, you may need to recommit to forgiveness over and over again.

Invariably when I speak on the subject of forgiveness, someone asks "what if I can't forgive?" Admittedly, forgiveness can be very challenging. It may be particularly hard to forgive someone who doesn't admit wrongdoing. Keep in mind that the key health benefits of forgiveness are *for you*, not the other person. If you find yourself challenged with forgiveness, it may be helpful to take some time to talk with a person you've found to be wise and compassionate, such as a spiritual leader, a healthcare provider, or an unbiased family member or friend. When all else fails, adopt the following mantra that I've used in the past: "I forgive. I release. I let go." Say it aloud as often as necessary. This mantra is one that I began using years ago. When confronted with an admixture of complex and powerful emotions, such as anger and resentment over an offense, I would quietly (and not so quietly) repeat to myself: "I forgive. I release. I let go." This statement uttered while interspersed with a few deep, cleansing, diaphragmatic breaths exerts a soothing, cathartic, and self-hypnotic effect. Said often enough, the mantra will persuade you to drop it—the emotional and spiritual load that unforgiveness would otherwise convince you to carry.

1. **Faith**. Believe in a power greater than yourself. When evaluating the practices of centenarians around the world, faith has been the one constant. It's not surprising. Belief and worship are written on the heart of every man, woman, boy and girl. That's why it is so easy to

become a fan (short for fanatic) of this or that. We were created to believe in someone or something greater than ourselves. So, exercise your faith. As a skill, faith is useful for patients, especially when managing a life-threatening illness, the complications and devastation of disease, and when implementing and supporting new lifestyle changes.

2. **Prayer and Meditation**. Prayer represents communication between the believer and her Higher Power. That communication may involve talking, expressions of praise, adoration and worship. Conversely, that spiritual communication may resemble listening and remaining silent in a receptive mode to receive divine ideas, imprints, and impressions.

Prayer is essential for a healthy spiritual life and for optimal spiritual wellness. Prayer and meditation are closely linked. Like prayer, meditation can also be described as a state of receptivity that fosters peace and multi-dimensional wellness, including the physical, spiritual, mental, and emotional realms. When practiced correctly, meditation is as potent as medication. It represents a calming and stilling of the mind that amplifies clarity of focus, thought, and intention. Meditation allows one to center herself and re-visit the source of her being, receiving new insights and inspiration. Meditation is an excellent catalyst for great creativity and heightened self-expression.

3. **Foster positive thoughts and vibrations**. Don't allow gossip, negative chatter and vibrations to enter your environmental space at work or at home. Foster positive thoughts and vibrations to elevate your experience of spiritual wellness.

Reflections

Reflections

Reflections

4. EMOTIONAL WELLNESS

As I described earlier, there is an interrelationship and interconnectedness of the different dimensions of wellness. As should be expected, with the emotional dimension of wellness, there's some overlap with the intellectual and spiritual domains of wellness. Our thoughts and emotions influence our health and well-being. Modern medicine is now recognizing the dynamic relationship between our emotions, our brain chemistry, and our physical bodies as evidenced by the disciplines of mind-body medicine and psychoneuroimmunology.

WISDOM AND STRATEGIES TO OPTIMIZE YOUR EMOTIONAL WELLNESS:

The lifestyle interventions that are proven to matter most when creating emotional wellness are:

Optimism. Optimistic individuals are cheerful and buoyant. When confronting obstacles, they know how to pivot and demonstrate great resiliency. All of these attributes conspire to yield better health outcomes for optimists. They tend to have lower levels of stress hormones and less inflammation in their bodies. Consequently, optimists are less likely to develop high blood pressure, heart disease, and chronic infections. They also tend to live longer than their pessimistic counterparts. More studies are needed to clarify the link between optimism and good health. However, it's likely that multiple mechanisms are involved. One of the leading reasons why optimism is associated with greater wellness is it appears that optimists build stronger social support networks.

Strong Social Networks: A wide network of support is of great benefit. As women in leadership, we naturally have an affinity for networks of people, such as sororities, professional associations, our churches and communities. Usually, in these instances, we're sharing our gifts and making contributions. However, in order to lead well, ladies, it's imperative that social support is bi-directional and that we're receiving encouragement, a listening ear, and nurturing from our closest relationships. Having a best friend that acts as a sounding board can be as advantageous as therapy or counseling. Establish a sister circle, a network of individuals you can rely on for prayer, encouragement, and advice.

Practice Good Sleep Hygiene: Go to bed at the same time every night. Remove ambient light and noise from your sleep environment as much as possible. Both noise and light in our sleep environment keep us from accessing deeper levels of rejuvenating sleep. It's important to secure at least six hours of sleep, preferably eight hours each night. When our sleep patterns are disrupted, we are more likely to become emotionally labile and experience volatile emotions such as anger, aggression, frustration, and irritability. If unchecked, these characteristics sabotage our efforts to lead well. So, establish a daily time to unplug from technology, decompress and get more rest.

Decrease Known Stressors. When our stress is reduced, we feel a greater sense of calm, peace, and emotional wellness.

Avoid excess sugar consumption. Is it a coincidence or not? Stressed spelled backwards is desserts. Excess sugar consumption can cause nervous system reactivity, irritability and anxiety, making the emotions labile. Additionally, excess sugar alters the body's pH, which should remain slightly alkaline at 7.42, leading to the depletions of vitamins and minerals and it contributes to the development of diabetes. Now, this isn't to say that all carbohydrate consumption is bad. Carbohydrates are a nutrient source along with proteins and fats. They are a healthy part of a balanced diet. Nevertheless, there is a misconception that all carbohydrates are bad for your health because some nutrient-scarce foods also fall into the category of carbohydrates such as doughnuts, cookies, cakes, candy, sodas, etc. However, the reality is, our bodies need carbohydrates such as whole grains, vegetables, fruits, and cooked dried beans and peas to sustain health and life. Choose your carbohydrates wisely and avoid excess sugar for optimal health. Dark chocolate is an excellent option and substitute for milk chocolate, which is found in most over-the-counter candies. It's loaded with phytonutrients, these plant-based chemicals, known as flavonoids. As a class of phytonutrients, flavonoids act as antioxidants neutralizing free radicals that would otherwise precipitate cellular damage throughout the body. Dark chocolate has less sugar than milk chocolate and it's rich in flavonoids. Let sweet treats be the exception to the rule, not the norm as you make your daily dietary choices.

Spirituality: Like stress reduction, a spiritual practice or expression of spirituality enhances feelings of emotional ease and mental harmony.

Ask for Help: Be willing to ask for help. It's a sign of emotional health and fortitude when we can ask for help when we need it. This is an area that I struggled in during my earlier life and leadership. I was challenged with displaying vulnerability and admitting that I needed assistance and support. Instead, I attempted to be Superwoman by doing it all, which led to career frustration and burnout. Those days are gone. Now, I ask for help all the time and I am willing to accept the gracious support of others. I realize no woman (or man) is an island. We need each other. The tasks, goals, and dreams we have in our lives are often not meant to be achieved alone. We were created for relationship and social interaction. Don't be afraid to ask for help. Your emotional self will thank you.

Adhere to the laws of balance and relaxation: Nature is inherently characterized by an ebb and flow. There's a rhythm to nature that's cyclical and seasonal. Our emotional health also depends on us striking a balance between work and rest. It is imperative to take a sabbatical, from time to time, away from the constant deluge of stimulation and stressors to recharge our emotional batteries. To really maximize our emotional wellness, we must learn and adhere to the laws of balance and relaxation. We must give ourselves time to think and just be. We are human-beings, not human-doings. However, so much of our time and daily schedules are consumed with doing and an incessant flurry of activities.

To relax is to engage our being-ness. Be with yourself and experience periodic solitude, even for just a few minutes a day. It will do wonders in recharging your emotional self. Be still. Eliminate unnecessary chatter and activity that's de-edifying. Sit and hear the sounds of nature. Sit and listen to your own thoughts. You'd be surprised how enlightening it can be to attend to one's own inner promptings and internal dialogue, which serve as the source of all external behaviors, drives, and impulses. If we can grasp an understanding of our inner motivation, we can often correct outer behaviors that threaten or sabotage our capacity to be well, and to lead well.

Aromatherapy: Involves the therapeutic use of botanical essences and essential oils like lavender, patchouli, lemongrass, sandalwood, etc. to ease certain symptoms, evoke peaceful and relaxing emotional states, and to heighten sense of well-being. Certain aromas and scents are healing to the body. The aroma of fresh flowers, a natural source of aromatherapy, can help you enjoy mental relaxation. Flowers promote relaxation. Reducing stress and maintaining low anxiety levels lead to an inner peace, which facilitates a greater degree of emotional wellness.

Be flexible and maintain a good attitude. Life is full of challenges and unknowns. From my experience, the best way to navigate rocky terrain in life is to be flexible and maintain a good attitude. When the unexpected occurs, keep your poise. Remain even tempered and you'll be able to generate creative solutions in the midst of even the most daunting circumstances and challenges.

Reflections

Reflections

Reflections

5. SOCIAL (OR RELATIONAL) WELLNESS

We have been created as social beings. We are meant to engage and interact with others in our environment in meaningful ways. This next dimension of wellness—social wellness—pertains to the relational realm and the well-being and quality of our relationships. The spectrum of quality relationships that comprise social wellness include healthy relationships with: one's self, one's Higher Power (spiritual wellness), one's significant other, family, friends, and co-workers (occupational wellness).

Being in harmonious relationships with others is critical to our overall experience of health and well-being since we spend so much of our time relating. There is never a moment when we are not relating. Even when we're alone, we're relating to ourselves and the inner landscape of our thoughts. We relate to our spouse, our children, our parents, our siblings, our colleagues, our neighbors, and perfect strangers. Because relationships comprise such a broad swath of our lives, we must carefully attend to this component of wellness. Successfully maneuvering the realm of relationships requires considerable skill and sensitivity. Successful leadership and social wellness is built on the foundation of emotional intelligence.

Emotional intelligence is the difference maker in quality relationships. The presence of emotional intelligence or the lack thereof can make or break the harmony in relationships. When possessed and used wisely, emotional intelligence can be a powerful skill for neutralizing conflict and breakdowns. It can also be a catalytic thrust for facilitating profound and immense breakthroughs in relationships.

Emotional intelligence (EQ) is not to be confused with intelligence or the intelligence quotient (IQ). IQ is a reference point for one's mental capacities and refers to the capability and ability to learn. Antithetically, emotional intelligence is "your ability to recognize and understand emotions in yourself and others, and your ability to use this awareness to manage your behavior and relationships". Emotional intelligence is a skill that can be learned. It affects how we manage behavior, navigate social complexities, and make personal decisions that achieve positive results. When it comes to leading well, emotional intelligence is the singular relational attribute that will escort you to the top of your industry and field. Emotional intelligence is the variable that explains success above and beyond one's IQ, education and credentials, and pedigree. Robust emotional intelligence is necessary for successful and effective leadership.

Emotional intelligence entered the vernacular of popular culture largely in part due to the success of Daniel Goleman's books on the subject. However, the concept of emotional intelligence is not new. In the field of psychology, emotional intelligence is regarded as a blend of several skills. At its core, emotional intelligence consists of four primary skills.[1]

1. Self-Awareness

2. Self-Management

3. Social Skills and Awareness

4. Relationship Management

Self-awareness is "your ability to accurately perceive your own emotions, while in the midst of relational interactions and activities, and understand your tendencies across these situations" (Bradberry & Greaves, 2009). It includes being attuned to your typical reactions to specific events, challenges and people.

Self-Management is "your ability to use your awareness of your emotions to stay flexible and direct your behavior positively. It is what happens when you act—or do not act."

Social Skills and Awareness is "your ability to accurately discern the emotions of other people and understand what is really going on with them. This level of awareness often means perceiving what other people are thinking and feeling, even if you do not feel the same way".

Relationship Management is "your ability to use your awareness of your own emotions and those of others to manage interactions successfully." This skill ensures clear communication and effective handling of conflict.

[1]*The above adapted from Bradberry, T., & Greaves, J. (2009). Emotional Intelligence 2.0. San Diego: TalentSmart.*

WISDOM AND STRATEGIES TO OPTIMIZE SOCIAL WELLNESS:

The lifestyle interventions that are proven to matter most when creating social wellness are:

1. **Master Emotional Intelligence.** It is such a worthwhile skill to build, that it will yield harmony among your constellation of family, friends, and associates as well as other huge relational gains. Keep a journal of your leadership experiences and how others respond to your leadership decisions. Learn from this data collection and become a more effective leader over time.

2. **Increase self-awareness.** To foster self-awareness, remember the following: avoid treating your feelings as good or bad. Your feelings are what they are, just observe them with neutrality. Get to know yourself under stress. Observe the ripple effect from your emotions. Know who and what serve as emotional triggers for you. Practice the aforementioned strategies for emotional wellness.

3. **Increase self-management.** During stressful situations, remember to breathe! In alignment with stress physiology, during periods of acute stress, our breathing

temporarily becomes rapid and shallow. When we are purposeful in our self-management of an episode of stress, diaphragmatic breathing deactivates the "fight or flight" response during acute stress and puts us in a more relaxed state of mind.

4. **Increase social awareness**: During social interactions, pay attention to body language, non-verbal gestures, and cues. People are always communicating, even when no words are being exchanged. Facial expression telegraphs a message. The eyes communicate. The use of certain hand gestures conveys a message. Pay attention to these non-verbal social cues. Another way to increase your social awareness, especially as a leader, is to greet people by name. It makes them feel special and acknowledged. Practice the art of listening. Lastly, practice empathy by imagining yourself in the other person's shoes.

5. **Increase relationship management capacities**: Demonstrate integrity at all times, which allows you to build trust with others. When you care, show it. Take opportunities to show your love and affinity for others every chance you get. Lastly, when involved in social interactions, align your intention with your impact.

Reflections

Reflections

Reflections

6. OCCUPATIONAL WELLNESS

As a professional woman in leadership, who has worked as many as 100 hours per week, I can honestly say that if occupational wellness is not achieved and maintained, it quickly leads to breakdowns in other areas of one's wellness experience. When occupational wellness is not present, typically social wellness is absent. With these two critical domains impacted, a lack of health and wholeness soon presents in the intellectual and physical dimensions as well. Financial wellness is invariably affected by these domains also. By now, hopefully, you get my point. Occupational wellness is foundational. For working adults, it is a springboard with direct access to the other dimensions of wellness. Think about it. We spend so much of our time at work. For the average person who works 40 hours per week, that totals 2,080 hours per year. If the average career spans 40 plus years, that's at minimum 83, 200 hours over the course of one's lifetime. Almost 100,000 hours, at minimum, is spent sowing your life's energy and work into the occupational dimension. One thing's for sure. The right occupation must be pursued—one that's in direct alignment with one's calling and purpose. When there is a mismatch in the occupational domain, and one is engaged in work that is devitalizing and energy-draining, there will be a complete derailment to the level of optimal health and wholeness that one can experience and achieve. This dimension of wellness requires serious soul-searching and self-reflection to truly get in touch with who you are and the unique talents and gifts that you are steward over for the purposes of serving the world.

WISDOM AND STRATEGIES TO OPTIMIZE YOUR OCCUPATIONAL WELLNESS:

The lifestyle interventions that are proven to matter most when creating occupational wellness are:

1. **Do what you love.** You get to decide how you serve the world and share your gifts. Again, self-reflection and soul searching are needed to identify the correct occupation and pursuits that are aligned with your purpose and best suit your talents and capabilities. Remember, don't consult what everyone else is doing. Do what you love. I speak from experience. I'm one of the few doctors that I know who has successfully branched out to pursue other career paths. Most doctors won't do it because of the heavy time and financial investments made during the process of becoming a doctor. They're constrained by their initial career choice. It takes courage to get off the beaten path and to try something new. However, it's worth it, ladies. Pursue what makes your heart sing and allows you to add value to others with joy.

2. **Find your tribe.** Identify kindred souls who are like-minded in your work, discipline, or specialty that will serve as a network of support as you go about your

occupational and executive duties. Your tribe will root for your growth and development and encourage you to become the best version of yourself by taking on new challenges and opportunities.

3. **Make sure that there are adequate periods of rest and respite from your vocational duties**. This measure helps you avoid burnout. Take a real vacation, not one where you take the office with you and end up answering emails and working on business projects. Power down. Minimize the use of electronics and enjoy your time away from the office so that you can fully rejuvenate and return to the office energized to take your leadership and occupational performance to the next level.

4. **Minimize conflict where possible at the workplace**. Use your emotional intelligence skill to help you navigate the occupational landscape and its scenarios.

Reflections

Reflections

Reflections

7. FINANCIAL WELLNESS

It's been said that there is no stress like debt stress. Financial worries tend to weigh heavy on the heart and soul and zap the joy out of living. The financial dimension of wellness is directly linked and parallel to all the other dimensions of wellness, including relational wellness. For instance, when we look at the divorce rate in our country, it's well over fifty percent (50 %). One of the number one reasons that marriages (or relationships in general) fail is related to finances. It's a fact. Money has a way of straining relationships, especially if one isn't personally evolved with enough emotional intelligence to avert this general pattern or tendency.

As a rule, I don't loan money that I can't afford to give away. In other words, if I loan money, it is because I can afford to give that amount of money away without creating financial strain or economic hardship. With this approach, worst case scenario, if I make a loan to a loved one or friend that is never repaid, there aren't sour feelings or a strained relationship that result. Instead, I extract the education from the experience so as not to repeat the error in the future.

To be financially well, one must be a good steward over finances. Oftentimes, it's not about pursuing or having more money, but it's about better managing the money we already have. The old adage is true. How you do anything is how you do everything. How you manage a dollar, is the same way you'll manage $100. How you manage $100 is the same way you'll manage a million. Managing money effectively requires discipline and trust, key skills for effective leadership. Take today to do an honest inventory of your status in this area. It's important and worthwhile to assess your financial management skills and to take the necessary steps to auto-correct and maximize your leadership and financial stewardship skills.

WISDOM AND STRATEGIES TO OPTIMIZE YOUR FINANCIAL WELLNESS:

The lifestyle interventions that are proven to matter most when creating financial wellness are:

1. **Pursue occupational alignment.** You must do meaningful work that is congruent with your passions. Only that which you are passionate about will you do well consistently, without fail. What you're passionate about, you'll do even if there's no compensation. Find the career path that ignites your passion and excites you. When you're impassioned and occupationally well suited, you will naturally pursue subject matter expert status in your field, industry, or discipline. As an expert, you will ultimately draw the financial compensation that is commensurate with your gifts, talents, and the game-changing contributions that you make.

2. **Don't allow money to strain your relationships.** Far too often, I've witnessed money matters destroy relationships. Because of the potential damage to human relations, it's advisable not to loan money. That's what banks are for. If possible, it's far better to sow a financial gift into the life of another rather than to make a loan.

However, in the off chance that you choose to make a loan, only loan money that you can afford to give away. If the money is returned, great. If not, consider it a gift and avoid loaning to that individual again. I can't emphasize enough that people are more important than money. The money is replaceable. People aren't. When confronted with a choice, always elect to preserve relationships.

3. **Handle debt stress with creative problem solving**. Try zero-based budgeting to help you track every dollar and penny that you earn and spend. Once you have assessed your spending patterns, you're able to make necessary adjustments to increase your financial viability and wellness. If expenses exceed income, look for opportunities to create other revenue streams. Leverage and monetize your skills in resourceful ways.

4. **Be a good steward of the financial resources entrusted to you**. Often, the barrier to greatness in the realm of finances is stewardship. As I stated previously, when it comes to increasing financial wellness, it's not that additional resources are necessarily needed, but wiser usage of resources is often required.

Reflections

Reflections

Reflections

Putting It All Together

In conclusion, be good to yourself. Each of the wellness dimensions must be nurtured and addressed in order to maximize wellness in every area of life. The strategies presented throughout this book are intended to help you bolster and amplify your capacity to lead well.

Lady Leaders, I specifically wrote this book with you in mind. The purpose of this book is to share the seven dimensions of wellness and interventions that are designed to facilitate greater vitality and an optimized sense of well-being. I intend for this book to shift the paradigm for how you perceive and experience wellness. Health is so much more than just being symptom free and disease free. The wellness dimensions and the associated interventions are the keys to inspired living and leadership with optimal joy. The wellness dimensions are platforms to explore and embrace new lifestyle strategies to restore balance, health, vitality and energy to the human body and its interactions. We are not just our parts. We are the sum total of our parts, so a holistic and integrative approach is necessary for achieving complete wellness and wholeness.

The utilization of this holistic approach facilitates the shift from a late-state disease orientation to a proactive primary prevention orientation. The late-state disease orientation often means that it is too late to stem the tide on the chronic diseases that claim countless lives and instead are relegated to the palliation of symptoms alone.

Preventive care is increasingly paramount to potentially decrease the morbidity and mortality from some of the most common chronic diseases that have perennially claimed the lives of women and all Americans, such as cardiovascular disease, cancer, diabetes, and stroke. Given the growing burden of chronic disease and the aging population that contemporary clinicians face in healthcare, utilization of the wellness dimensions and a holistic health approach is going to become increasingly important. Hopefully, this book leaves you better than it found you, well equipped with the strategies and interventions to lead well and be well.

About the Author

Dr. Paula Walker King (Dr. Paula) is a board-certified physician, speaker, and women's leadership coach. She helps women in power elevate their career and manage their personal challenges in order to experience a full and abundant life. Dr. Paula completed her Bachelor of Science degree at Howard University and her Master of Public Health at Emory University. She achieved her medical degree at Wayne State University School of Medicine, completing her post-doctoral residency at St. John Hospital & Medical Center.

Dr. Paula is passionate about health promotion and using evidence-based methods to prevent disease and to stay healthy naturally. Dr. Paula has presented extensively on prevention science and health and wellness. She is a contributor on WTVM, an ABC television affiliate in Columbus, Georgia, where she writes and hosts a weekly TV health segment. In her spare time, Dr. Paula enjoys shopping, traveling, and spending time with her husband and son.

To learn more, visit her website at
DrPaulaMD.com

CREATING DISTINCTIVE BOOKS WITH INTENTIONAL RESULTS

We're a collaborative group of creative masterminds with a mission to produce high-quality books to position you for monumental success in the marketplace.

Our professional team of writers, editors, designers, and marketing strategists work closely together to ensure that every detail of your book is a clear representation of the message in your writing.

Want to know more?
Write to us at info@publishyourgift.com
or call (888) 949-6228

Discover great books, exclusive offers, and more at
www.PublishYourGift.com

Connect with us on social media

@publishyourgift

www.ingramcontent.com/pod-product-compliance
Lightning Source LLC
Chambersburg PA
CBHW052056070526
44584CB00017B/2209